HORSES & PONIES

Illustrated by
Carrie Fink

Kidsbooks®

Manufactured in China

0407-3C

Visit us at **www.kidsbooks.com®**

INTRODUCTION

This book will show you how to draw lots of horses and ponies. What is the difference between a horse and a pony? Ponies are horses—just smaller. A pony is a breed of horse that is shorter than 58 inches, measured at the shoulder. A Shetland pony may be just 40 inches tall, while a Clydesdale will be 60 to 72 inches tall.

You will find many different kinds of horses and ponies in this book. Some will be more difficult to draw than others, but if you follow along, step by step, you soon will be able to draw horses, ponies, and many other kinds of four-legged animals.

Each drawing in this book begins with several basic shapes, usually a combination of ovals and simple lines. Variations of other basic shapes and lines are used to connect the shapes. Using these basic shapes will help you start your drawing.

SUPPLIES

NUMBER-2 PENCILS	**FELT-TIP PEN**
SOFT ERASER	**COLORED PENCILS**
DRAWING PAD	**MARKERS OR CRAYONS**

HELPFUL HINTS

1. Take your time with steps 1 and 2. Following the first steps carefully will make the final steps easier. The first two steps create a solid foundation of the animal—much like a builder who must first construct a foundation before building the rest of the house. Next comes the fun part: creating the smooth, clean outline of the horse, then adding all the finishing touches, such as details, shading, and color.

2. Keep your pencil lines light and soft. This will make your guidelines easier to erase when you no longer need them.

3. Don't be afraid to erase. It usually takes a lot of drawing and erasing before you will be satisfied with the way your drawing looks. Each horse has special characteristics that will make it easier or, in some cases, harder to draw. However, it is easier to draw anything if you break it down into simple shapes.

4. Leave the details, shading, and all other finishing touches for last. Put them in only *after* you have blended and refined all the shapes and your figure is complete.

5. Remember: Practice makes perfect. Don't be discouraged if you don't get the hang of it right away. Just keep drawing, erasing, and redrawing until you do.

PARTS OF A HORSE

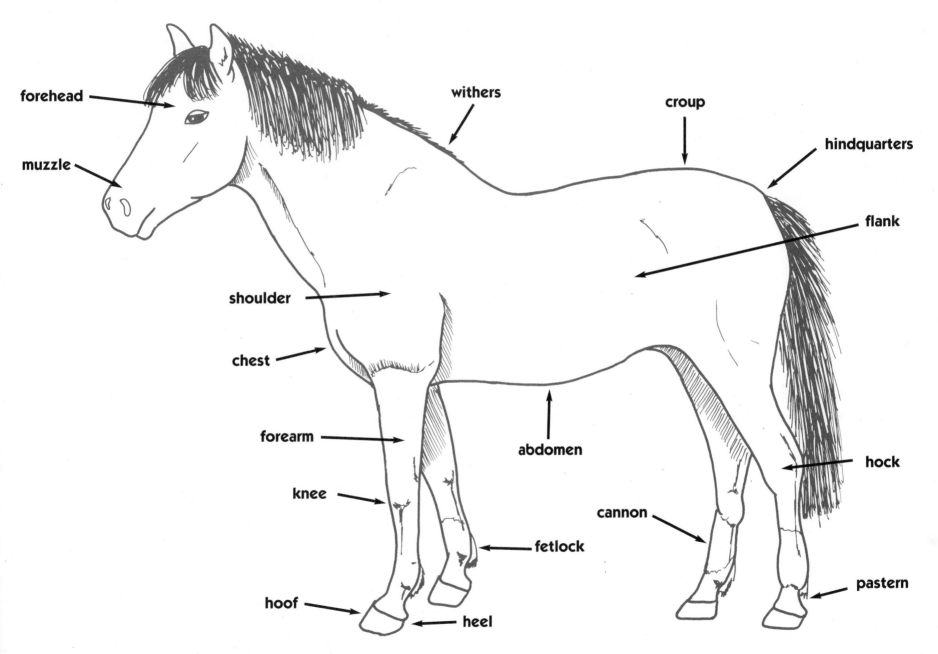

forehead

muzzle

withers

croup

hindquarters

flank

shoulder

chest

forearm

abdomen

hock

knee

cannon

fetlock

pastern

hoof

heel

HOW TO START

Step 1. Begin by drawing a few basic shapes (usually ovals), such as the ones in step 1 below. This creates a rough outline of the horse's head and body. Dotted lines represent guidelines that you will erase when you no longer need them (in this case, in steps 2 and 3).

Step 2. Sketch and erase to add legs and refine the horse's body shape. Then draw new guideline shapes (ovals, again) to start the legs. You now have the basic structure of a horse. In the next two steps, you will build on this foundation.

Step 3. Start adding other major horse features, such as the mane, tail, and hooves. Work carefully to blend all the lines and shapes into a smooth, clean outline drawing.

Step 4. Continue to refine your drawing as you fill in the final details. When your horse is complete, add your favorite colors or, for a more dramatic effect, outline it with a thick black marker.

Feel free to make some details, such as face and body markings, different from the ones shown here. You also may want to add backgrounds. (You will find some scenery on pages 90-91.) After you have drawn some or all of the horses and ponies in this book and are comfortable with your drawing technique, try drawing these and other kinds of animals on your own.

Remember: It is not important to get it perfect. It *is* important for you to be happy with your work!

ERASING TIPS

- Once you have completed the line drawing (usually after steps 2 and 3), erase all unneeded guidelines.
- A very soft or kneaded eraser will erase the pencil lines without smudging the drawing or ripping the paper.

- Using a permanent, fine-line marker over pencil lines you want to keep (at the end of step 3) will make it easier to erase any leftover guidelines.
- Remember: Erasing is an important part of the process!

 1.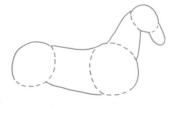

2.

3.

4.

HEAD (side view)

In many of the drawings in this book, the head is the most detailed part of the animal. Before you get started on whole horses, get some practice by drawing this head and the one on the next page.

1. Using soft, light pencil strokes, draw an oval to start the head. Add a *U*-shape to serve as a muzzle guideline.

2. Next, draw two lines for the neck and add two small triangles for the ears. Erase any guidelines you no longer need.

3. Working carefully on one area at a time, erase lines you don't need as you add new ones. Add a mane and an eye. Reshape the muzzle, adding a nostril and mouth.

4. Draw the final details: the hairs of the mane, the eyelid and darkened eye, contour (shaping) lines on the muzzle, and shading. You are done!

HEAD (front view)

Some horses and ponies have markings on their faces. Each type of marking has its own name. When you get to step 4 of this face, you can draw the same marking we did, or choose one from the next page.

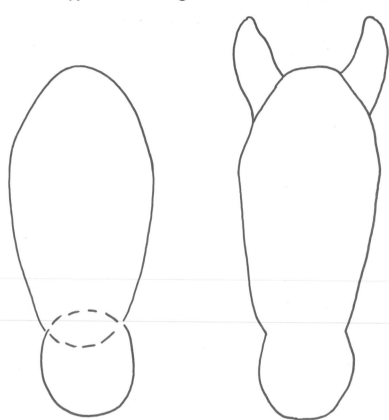

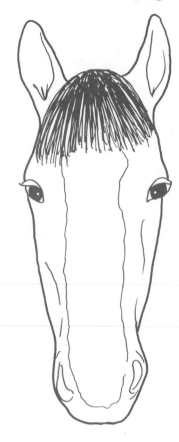

1. Start the face with a long, narrow oval. Overlapping that, draw a smaller, rounder oval.

2. Erase the lines between the two ovals. At the top, draw shapes (like curving triangles) for the ears, as shown.

3. Erase and redraw to refine the shape of the face as you add eyes and nostrils. Draw a jagged line for the mane.

4. Now add the final details, including the folds of the ears and the hair of the mane. Draw the marking last.

TYPES OF FACE MARKINGS

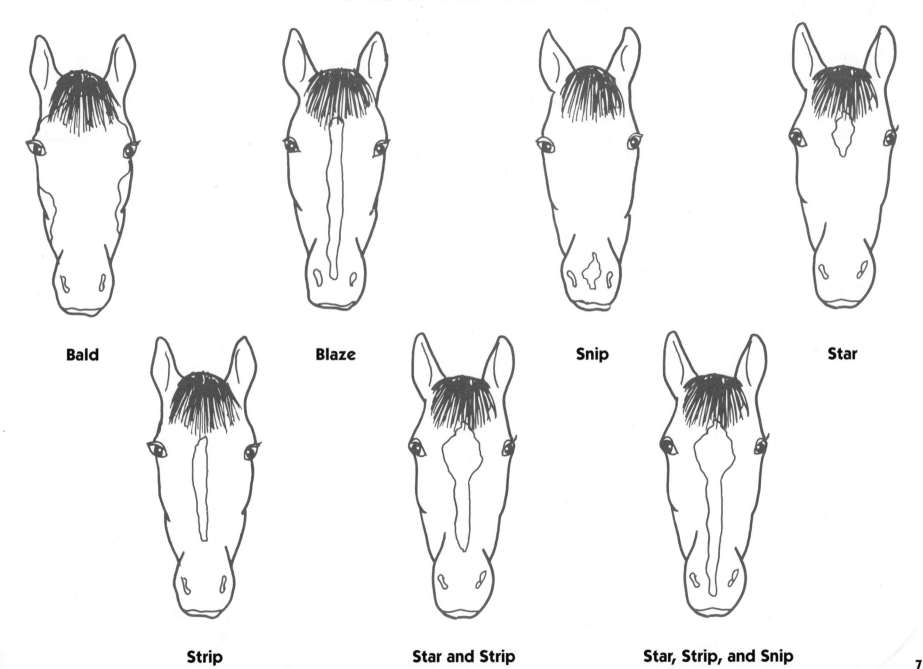

Bald

Blaze

Snip

Star

Strip

Star and Strip

Star, Strip, and Snip

7

Hanoverian

The Hanoverian *(han-oh-VEER-ee-un)* horse was bred in 1735 in northern Germany. Today, this horse, which can be found all over the world, is one of the most popular riding horses. The Hanoverian can be any solid color, such as brown or black, but some have white "socks" and face markings.

Tip: Always keep your pencil lines light and soft, so that guidelines will be easy to erase when you no longer need them.

1. Start by drawing three ovals: a large one for the shoulders, a slightly smaller one for the hindquarters, and a small one for the head. Then connect the ovals, as shown.

2. Erase unneeded lines as you erase and resketch to shape the head. Then add small ovals and simple lines to create the legs and hooves.

3. Create the ears, eyes, muzzle, and mane. Then erase unneeded guidelines to refine the legs and hooves. Don't forget to add the tail! Do not go on to the last step until you are satisfied with your step 3 drawing.

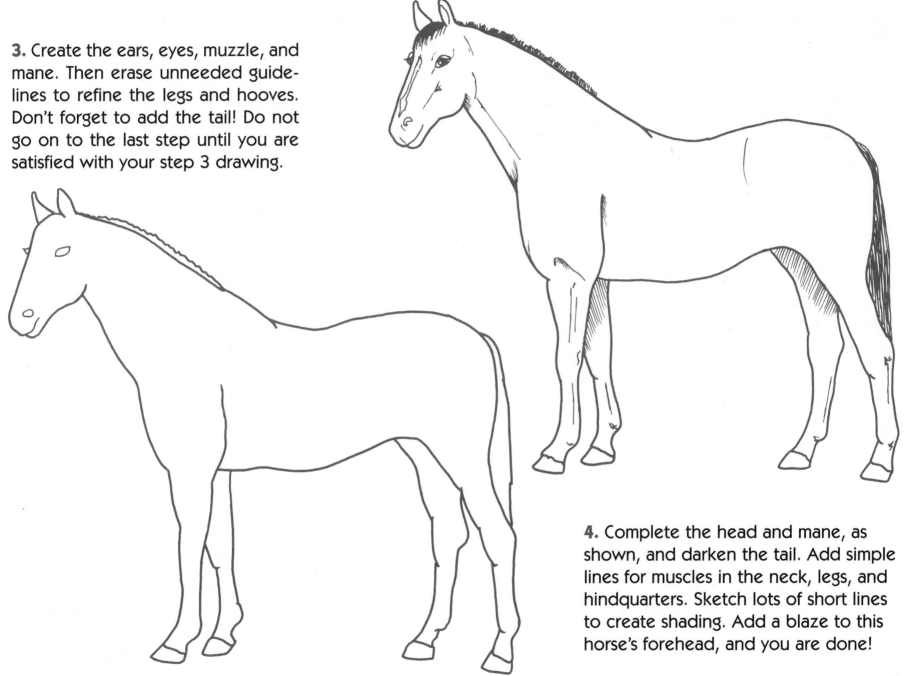

4. Complete the head and mane, as shown, and darken the tail. Add simple lines for muscles in the neck, legs, and hindquarters. Sketch lots of short lines to create shading. Add a blaze to this horse's forehead, and you are done!

Morgan

The Morgan is the first documented American horse breed. It has been used as a workhorse, a city horse, and a racing horse. The Morgan was used by miners during the California gold rush of 1849 and by troops in the Civil War (1861-1864). Morgans are found in many colors, including brown, chestnut (reddish brown), black, gray, and yellow.

Tip: Dotted lines represent guidelines that you will erase later, when you no longer need them.

1. Draw two large circles close together, as shown, and connect them to form the horse's body. Add a smaller oval above, then connect them to create the neck and muzzle.

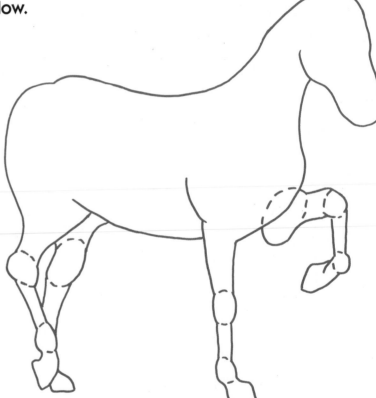

2. Erase guidelines to refine the shape of the horse's head and body. Then use simple lines and shapes to create the legs and hooves.

3. Take your time with this step. Working on one area at a time, add the eyes, nostril, and mouth. Then erase and redraw to form the ears and mane. Next, add a tail, then work on the legs and hooves.

4. Darken the mane and tail. Adding muscle lines and shading will give the Morgan a 3-D look. Your high-stepping Morgan will soon be on its way!

Shetland Pony

The Shetland pony may be the oldest horse breed of Great Britain. It comes from the Shetland Islands, which lie in a chilly area off the northern coast of Scotland. Shetland ponies have thick, shaggy fur that keeps them warm. Their coats are all horse colors and patterns, except spotted. Originally, in the 1800s, they often were used to do work, such as hauling coal cars out of mines. Today, they often are pets and pull small carriages.

Tip: Steps 1 and 2 establish the overall structure and look of your drawing. Take the time to get them just right before going on to steps 3 and 4.

1. Start by drawing two overlapping circles, for the head and shoulders. Add a third circle for the hindquarters. Then draw connecting lines for the neck, muzzle, and body.

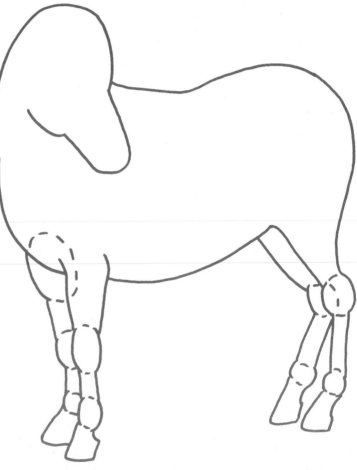

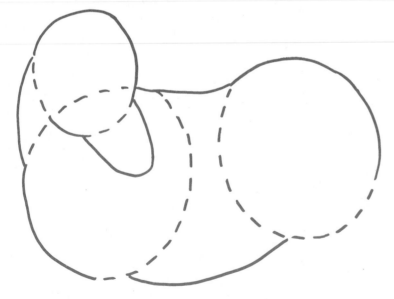

2. Sketch and erase to clean up the head and body. Then add guideline shapes for the legs and hooves.

3. Sketch and erase to make smooth, clean outlines of the the legs and hooves. Use simple lines and shapes to start the ears, facial features, mane, and tail.

4. Note this pony's body markings. Use lots of little dots to create the markings, as shown. Finish the ears and facial features, then finish the legs and hooves. (Notice the shape of this pony's fetlocks, and the tufts of hair on them.) Finish up by using lots of long, dark lines to give the mane and tail a thick, shaggy look.

fetlock

Tennessee Walking Horse

This breed is known for its unusual gait (way of walking). Southern plantation owners of the 1800s, who used these horse on their large farms, called them "Plantation Walkers." Today, this animals is used as a trail or show horse. It usually is brown, black, white, reddish, or gray, but its face, legs, and body may also have white coloring.

1. Draw a large oval for the shoulders, then add smaller ones for the hips and head. Add a muzzle and neck, and connect the shoulders and hips to form the body.

2. Erase unneeded guidelines as you reshape the head and add another oval for the top of the rear leg. Next, take your time adding the legs as shown. (Note the bend in the rear legs, and the straightness and position of the front legs.)

3. Clean up the body and legs, erasing old guidelines and refining the shapes. Add guideline shapes and lines for the eyes, nostril, and mouth. Create the ears. Then add the windblown mane and the tail with its curving twist. Use jagged lines to make the ends of the mane and tail look shaggy.

4. Complete the ears and facial features. Then add the final details: darken the mane, add shading to give the picture depth, and draw curving lines to show the muscles in this horse's neck, chest, and legs.

Welsh Mountain Pony

This breed was originally found in the hills and valleys of Wales, in Great Britain. Its coat is black, gray, cream, or brown. Welsh ponies have worked in coal mines, on ranches, and have carried the mail.

Tip: It is easy to draw almost anything if you first break it down into simple shapes.

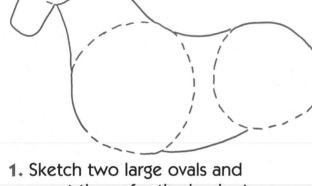

1. Sketch two large ovals and connect them, for the body. A smaller oval and three simple lines create the pony's head, muzzle, and neck.

2. Using small ovals and simple lines, create the legs. Add the tail. Then erase unneeded guidelines as you reshape the head and add eyes, ears, mane, nostril, and mouth.

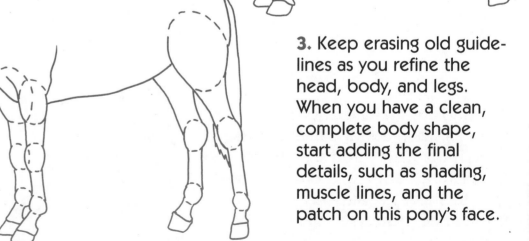

3. Keep erasing old guidelines as you refine the head, body, and legs. When you have a clean, complete body shape, start adding the final details, such as shading, muscle lines, and the patch on this pony's face.

16

Foal

A foal is a young horse, male or female, that is under one year of age.

Tip: If at any point you don't like the way something looks, erase it and try it again.

1. First, create the body, as shown. Then add guidelines for the head and neck.

2. Sketching lightly and erasing guidelines you don't need, reshape the head and body, adding the tail, mane, and facial features. Then add the legs, working on one at a time.

3. Now it is time to add the finishing touches to this frisky youngster. Adding shading and contour lines will make this foal pop off your page!

Chincoteague Pony

The Chincoteague (*shing-kuh-TEEG*) pony lives on Assateague Island in Chincoteague Bay, off the coasts of Maryland and Virginia. Experts think that these animals were brought to the U.S. from Europe 300 years ago. When the ship sank, the ponies swam to the island and have lived there, in the wild, ever since. These ponies are found in many colors. They often have pinto markings—a solid color with large patches of white.

Tip: Before you start, study the step 4 drawing. This will help you understand what you will be doing in steps 1, 2, and 3.

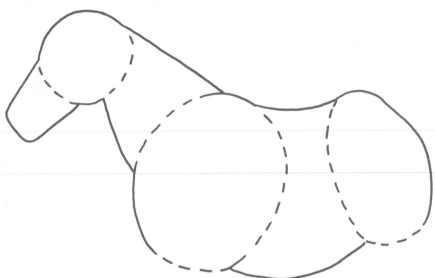

1. Draw a big oval for this pony's chest, and a smaller irregular one for its hindquarters. Join them to create the body. (Notice how the back and belly curve.) Then add the head and neck, as shown.

2. Sketch and erase to shape and smooth this pony's head and body into a clean outline drawing. Then add guideline shapes for the legs and hooves.

4. Darken the tail and mane. (Remember to draw the fringe of mane hanging on the far side of this pony's neck!) Next, add shading and muscle lines to give your drawing depth. Finally, use lots of dark, tiny dots or colored pencils or markers to add markings to this animal's coat. This is *your* pony, so make its dark patches any size or shape you like!

3. Working on one leg at a time, erase unneeded guidelines and make a clean outline. Do the same for the head, adding ears, a mane, eye, nostril, and mouth. Erase and resketch until you are happy with each part, as well as the overall drawing.

Pinto

A pinto is a horse or pony with a coat with patches of white and another color. (*Pinto* is a Spanish word meaning "painted.") An *overo* pinto has a dark coat with white spots. A *tobiano* pinto has a white coat with dark spots. Native Americans of the West often rode pintos into war, because the animals' coloring made good camouflage.

1. This pinto is rearing on its hind legs, so draw the oval for the shoulders higher than the oval for the hindquarters, as shown. Connect those two basic shapes, then add the head and neck.

2. Erase unneeded guidelines as you reshape the head and body. Then add guideline shapes for the legs, sketching the rear legs first.

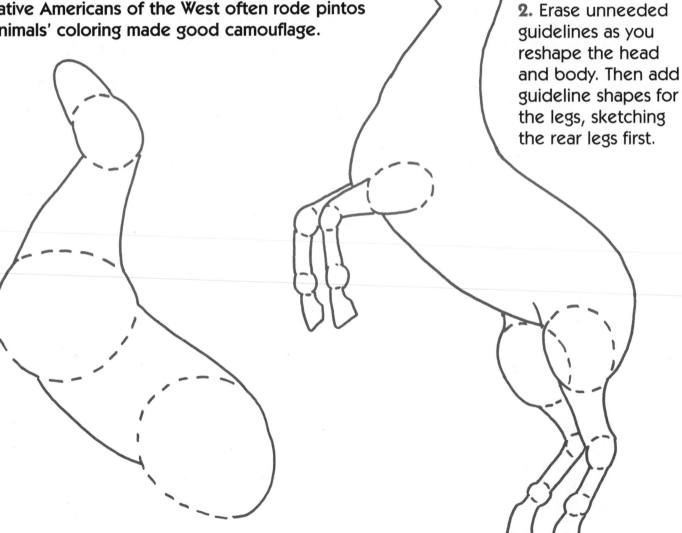

3. Erase unneeded lines as you work. Add ears and facial features as you refine the shape of the head. Add the mane. Then refine the body and legs until you have a clean, smooth outline drawing of the pinto.

Tip: Add details and all the finishing touches only *after* your figure is complete.

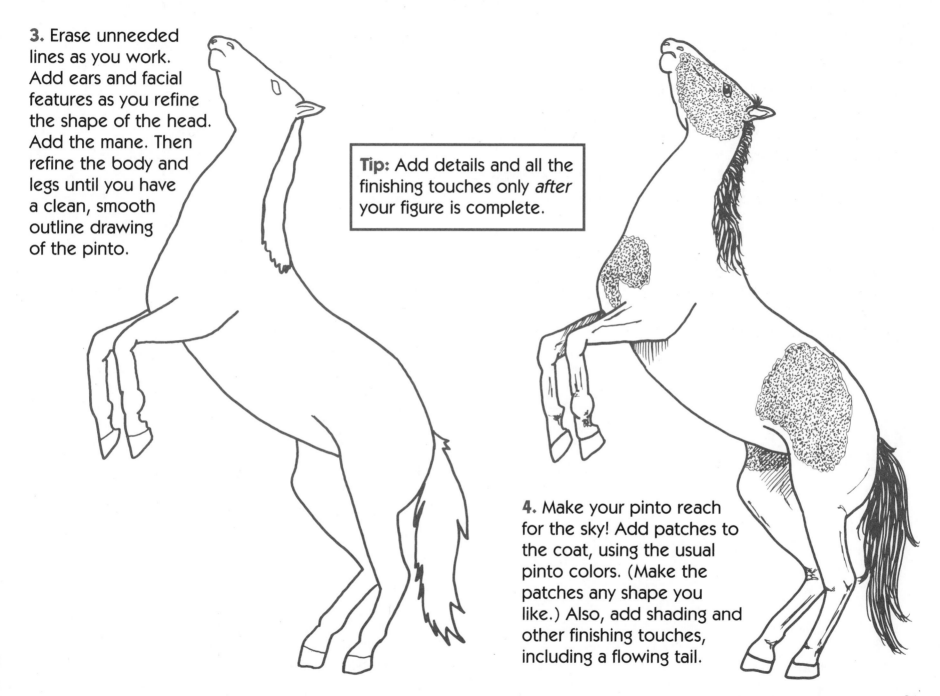

4. Make your pinto reach for the sky! Add patches to the coat, using the usual pinto colors. (Make the patches any shape you like.) Also, add shading and other finishing touches, including a flowing tail.

Sorraia

The Sorraia *(sor-EYE-yuh)* is a wild horse, first found in Portugal in 1920. This horse has a much earlier history: It has been found drawn in prehistoric cave art. Today, the Sorraia is nearly extinct. Most live in Portugal and Germany. All Sorraias are dun (grayish yellow) or gray, often with dark stripes on their sides and legs.

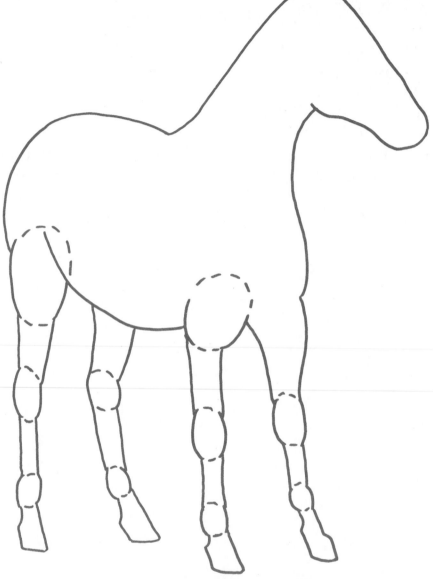

1. Sketching lightly, draw one large oval for the body, and a smaller oval for the head. Connect them for a neck. Add the muzzle.

2. For each leg, sketch several ovals, then connect them, as shown. Reshape the head, erasing guidelines as you work.

3. Take your time creating the ears and mane. Add the facial features, including the curving jawline. Next, refine the shape of the body and legs. Add the tail.

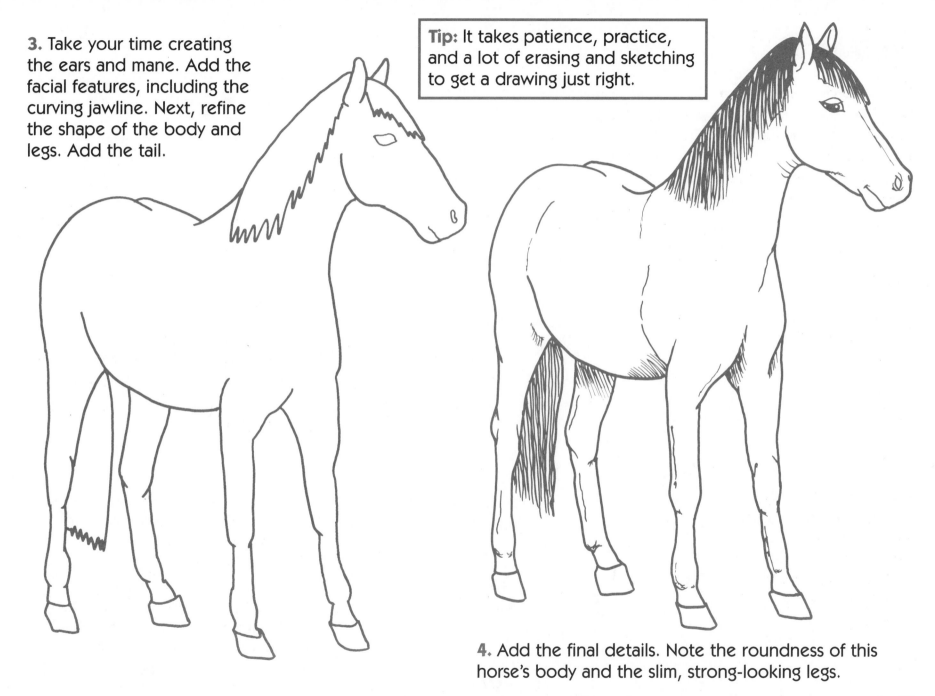

Tip: It takes patience, practice, and a lot of erasing and sketching to get a drawing just right.

4. Add the final details. Note the roundness of this horse's body and the slim, strong-looking legs.

Shire

This gray or black-and-white English horse is used as a working horse, since it is very strong and can pull a lot of weight. In 1924, a pair of Shire horses pulled a load that weighed 45 tons. (That is equal to 5 full-grown African elephants!)

1. First, draw three ovals, as shown. Then add connecting lines to form this horse's head, neck, and body. (Dotted lines show what you will erase later.)

2. Reshape the head and body, erasing what you no longer need. Then sketch ovals with connecting lines to form this horse's legs and hooves.

Tip: If this horse seems difficult to draw, look for the simple shapes in each area. Then take your time, working carefully on one section at a time. You will find that you can do it, after all!

3. Erase and redraw until the legs and hooves are the way you want them. (Note how thick they are at the bottom.) Rework the head and neck to add ears, mane, and facial features. Then add chest muscle lines and a tail.

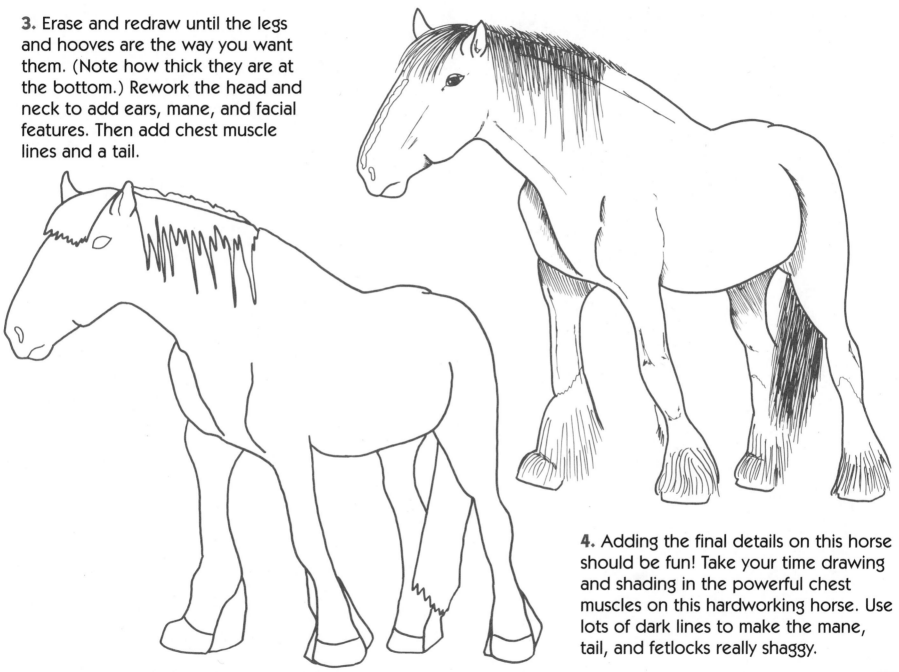

4. Adding the final details on this horse should be fun! Take your time drawing and shading in the powerful chest muscles on this hardworking horse. Use lots of dark lines to make the mane, tail, and fetlocks really shaggy.

Quarter Horse

One of the oldest horse breeds in North America, quarter horses were used for a variety of things, including farming, rounding up cattle, and hauling lumber. English settlers raced them over quarter-mile stretches, which is how the breed became known as the "quarter-mile" or the quarter horse. This horse can be found in many different colors, but reddish brown is the most common.

1. Start by drawing guideline shapes for the chest, hindquarters, and head. Connect those shapes to form this horse's muzzle, neck, and body.

Remember: Keep all your lines lightly drawn in the first steps, so they will be easy to erase when you need to.

2. Erase unneeded head and body guidelines, then sketch new ones to create the legs. Take care with this step, noting how each leg of this running horse is bent.

3. Keep erasing and resketching to reshape the head, body, and legs. Add mane, tail, and facial features. Before going on to step 4, make sure that you have a smooth, clean outline drawing of the quarter horse—and are satisfied with it.

4. This horse has strong legs. As you add the finishing touches, be sure to highlight the muscles in the legs and chest. Have fun with the flowing mane and tail. Don't forget the marking on the forehead!

Przewalski's Horse

Przewalski's horse is also known as the Asian wild horse. It is the last wild subspecies of horse. In North America, there are only about 150 of these horses, and almost all are in zoos. This horse has a dark mane and tail, and its coat is yellowish or light red.

Tip: It is easy to draw almost anything if you first build a good foundation.

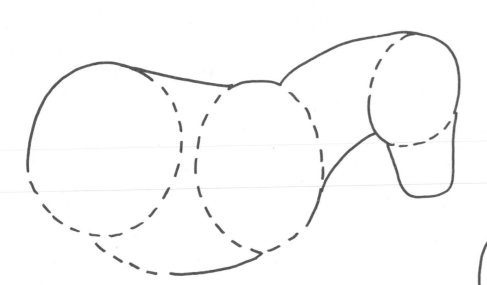

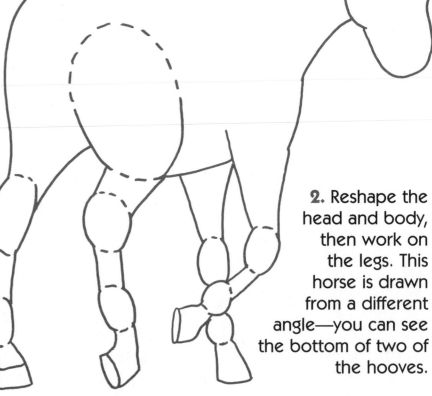

1. Starting with the largest shape first, draw guideline shapes for the body and head, then connect them as shown. Take note of the way the lines of the neck and belly curve.

2. Reshape the head and body, then work on the legs. This horse is drawn from a different angle—you can see the bottom of two of the hooves.

3. Create ears and a mane, then add facial features. Draw in the swishing tail before refining the body and legs.

4. Use lots of short, dark lines to add hair to the fetlocks and give the mane a brushy look. Add shading and curving contour lines to highlight this wild horse's muscular body.

Fell Pony

The Fell pony is native to northern England. (*Fell* is an Old English word that means "hill.") This strong, friendly pony once herded sheep, carried miners' packs, and ran races. Today, it often carries riders or runs free in the hills. The Fell pony's coat is black, brown, bay (reddish brown with a black mane and tail), or gray.

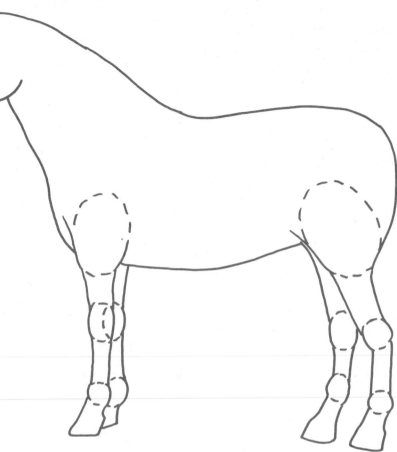

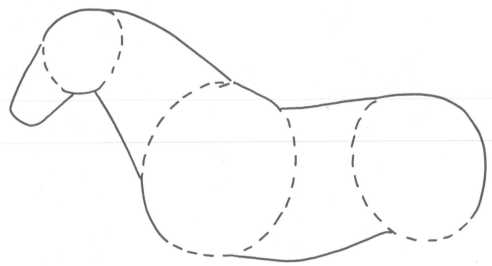

1. Sketch the basic shapes for the body and head, then connect them. Add the muzzle.

2. Draw and erase to reshape the head. Do the same for the body. Then add guideline shapes for the legs and hooves.

Remember: Studying the step 4 drawing before you start will help you understand how the basic shapes relate to each other.

3. Create ears and add the long, shaggy mane. Sketch in guideline shapes for the eye, nostril, and mouth. Add the long tail, then focus on refining the shapes of the body and legs.

4. Now it is time to add all the final details and finishing touches—including the long, shaggy mane and hairy fetlocks. Which of the four colors will *your* Fell pony be?

Dutch Warmblood

The Dutch Warmblood, which is from the Netherlands, is a sport horse. It is entered into competitions, such as jumping. This horse is chestnut (reddish brown with a brown mane and tail), bay (reddish brown with a black mane and tail), black, or gray. Many have white markings on the face and legs.

1. Start by drawing two ovals for the chest and hindquarters. Take note of the way each oval is angled. Then add the head and connecting lines for the neck and body.

Remember: Steps 1 and 2 are very important. They establish the overall structure and look of your drawing.

2. Erase unneeded guidelines as you reshape the head and body, and begin sketching in the legs and hooves.

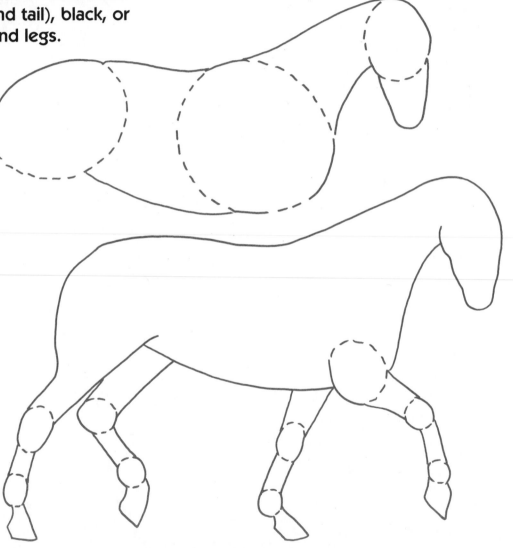

3. Sketch in the ears, mane, and facial features as you reshape the head and neck. Add the tail before refining the shapes of the body and each leg. Be patient and take your time with this step!

4. Use lots of long, flowing dark lines to finish the tail. With lots of short, dark lines, add shading that will give this horse's body a 3-D look. Be sure to define the fetlocks and leg muscles of this strong, graceful animal.

Appaloosa

This American spotted horse was used by the Oregon American Indians in the 1700s. It is a descendant of the first horses in North America, brought by Spanish explorers. The Appaloosa has a distinctive coat: white with dark spots all over, a color with white spots all over, or a solid color with a white patch and small spots on its hips.

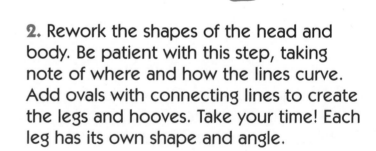

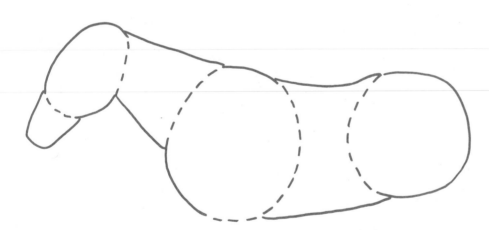

1. Lightly sketch three ovals, as shown, then connect them to form the neck and body. Add a simple guideline shape for the muzzle. (Dotted lines show what you will erase in the next step.)

2. Rework the shapes of the head and body. Be patient with this step, taking note of where and how the lines curve. Add ovals with connecting lines to create the legs and hooves. Take your time! Each leg has its own shape and angle.

3. Erasing lines you no longer need, sketch in ears and a mane. Add the eye and facial features, then the tail. Then rework the body and legs until you have a clean outline drawing.

Remember: Focus on one area at a time, sketching and erasing until you are satisfied with it.

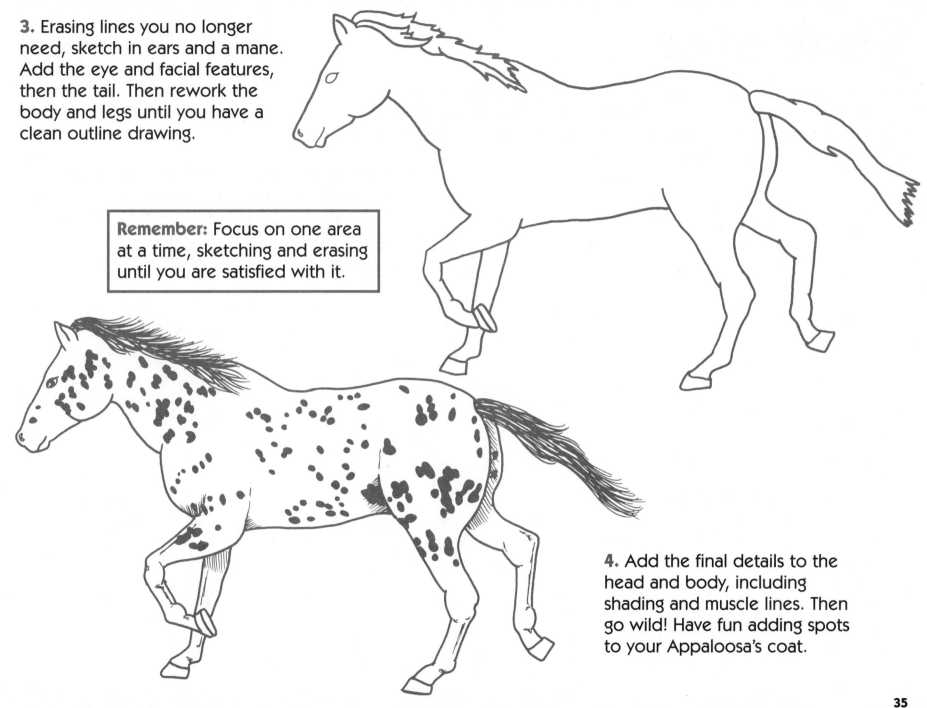

4. Add the final details to the head and body, including shading and muscle lines. Then go wild! Have fun adding spots to your Appaloosa's coat.

Haflinger

The Haflinger originated in the area of Hafling, a village that was in Austria until 1919, when it became part of Italy. The Haflinger, which is a common farm pony in Europe, has a light-brown coat with pale, straw-colored mane and tail.

2. Erase unneeded guidelines as you shape the head and body into a clean outline. Then draw ovals and lines, as shown, to add the legs. The front legs are curved, because this horse is running.

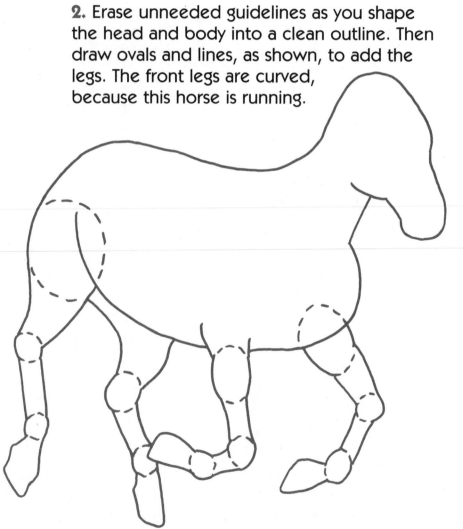

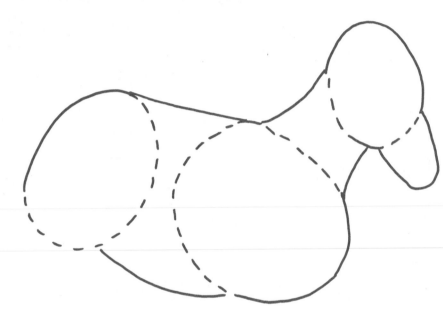

1. Start by lightly sketching ovals for the chest and hindquarters, then connect them. (Note the different angles of the two ovals.) Add an oval for the head, two connecting lines to form the neck, and a *U*-shaped line for the muzzle.

3. First, focus on the head. Erase old lines as you create the ears and shaggy mane, and add facial features. Then work on the body and the legs, erasing and redrawing until you are satisfied. Don't forget to add a tail!

Remember: Add details and all the finishing touches *after* your figure is complete.

4. Fill in the details of the head and facial features. Add shading and contour lines to highlight the muscles in this horse's body and legs. Your Haflinger will be hot to trot!

American Saddlebred

The American Saddlebred—also known as the American saddle horse—became famous during the Civil War (1861-1865). Many famous generals of that war, such as Robert E. Lee, Ulysses S. Grant, and Stonewall Jackson, rode it. This horse is a blend of several breeds, including the Arabian, Morgan, and Thoroughbred. Its coat is usually a solid color with white markings.

1. Draw two large ovals for the chest and hindquarters, then connect them. (Allow enough room between the two for this horse's long body.) Add the head and neck.

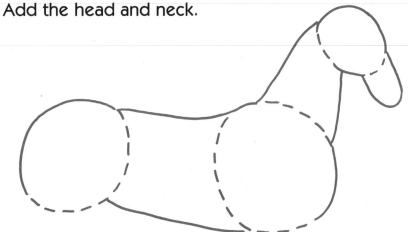

2. Keeping only the lines you need, erase and redraw to shape the head and body. Then sketch ovals and simple lines to start the legs and hooves.

3. Working on one area at a time, create a clean, smooth outline drawing of the horse, including the mane, ears, facial features, hooves, and long, flowing tail.

Tip: Once you are satisfied with your step 3 drawing, use a fine-point pen or marker over lines you want to keep. This will make it easier to erase any guidelines that remain.

4. To make this proud horse stride right off the page, add details that add depth and perspective. Filling in muscle lines on the legs and chest will help accomplish this—so will shading on the chest and far legs. Use long, flowing pencil or marker strokes when you add the finishing touches to the mane and tail.

Bashkir

The Bashkir is a small horse with a large head and short neck. It originally was used as a workhorse in northern Eurasia, near the Ural Mountains. (Bashkir is a region of Russia.) Most Bashkir horses are roan (black, brown, or red, with lots of white hairs mixed in), with white markings. Others are gray, brown, or black.

Tip: Practice makes perfect. Don't be discouraged if you don't get the hang of it right away. Just keep drawing and erasing until you do.

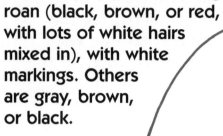

1. Start by lightly drawing two large, overlapping ovals, as shown. Connect them to form the body. Then add shapes for the neck, head, and muzzle.

2. Continue the neck lines upward as you erase unneeded guidelines. Refine the shape of the head and body, then add the legs. (The rear legs overlap.)

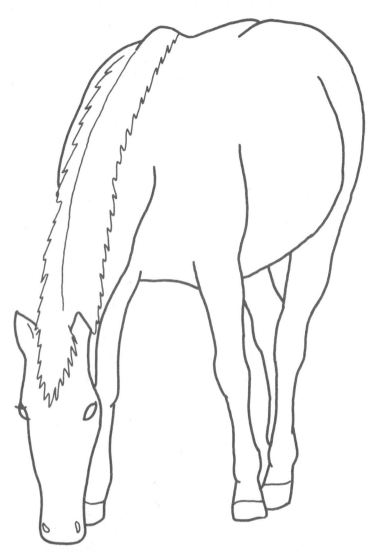

3. Add guideline shapes for the nostrils, eyes, ears, and mane. (This is an interesting angle for seeing and drawing the mane.) Erase and redraw to refine the shape of the body and legs. Add hooves.

4. Add shading to the legs and body, especially along muscle lines and folds in the skin. Making some lines thick and other lines thin will help add depth, too. Fill in the mane, refine the ears and eyes, and add the forehead marking. Then give your Bashkir some grass to eat!

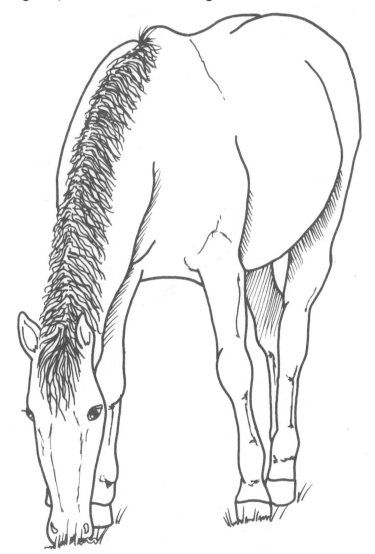

Falabella

The Falabella is the smallest pony in the world. It grows from 28 to 32 inches tall. That is under 3 feet—shorter than the knob on a door! This horse, named for breeder Julio Falabella of Argentina, is usually brown or black, but comes in other colors as well.

1. Draw a large oval for the chest and shoulders, then a somewhat smaller one for the hindquarters. Connect them. Next, sketch guideline shapes for the head and muzzle, and draw a neck connecting them to the body.

2. Erase unneeded guidelines in the body, then draw new ones for the legs and hooves. Reshape the head.

3. Refine the shape of the head and add facial features. Sketch and erase to make the ears and mane. Next, clean and reshape the body and legs. Then add the long, full tail.

Tip: If something looks complex, focus on one part at a time. Look for simple, basic shapes, even when adding final details.

4. Put in all the final details. Darken the eye, mane, and tail. (Use lots of lines in the mane and tail, as if each line were a hair.) Add skin wrinkles, muscle lines, and shadows. Spotted Falabellas are rare, but we made ours a rare one! Do the same, or make yours your own.

Colt

A colt is a young male horse.

Remember: Studying the step 4 drawing before you begin will help you understand how the guideline shapes fit together.

1. Keeping your lines light and softly drawn, sketch two ovals, just barely touching one another. Add guideline shapes for the head, then connect the shapes as shown.

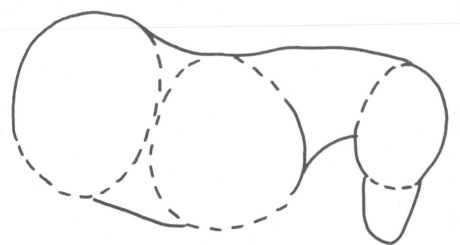

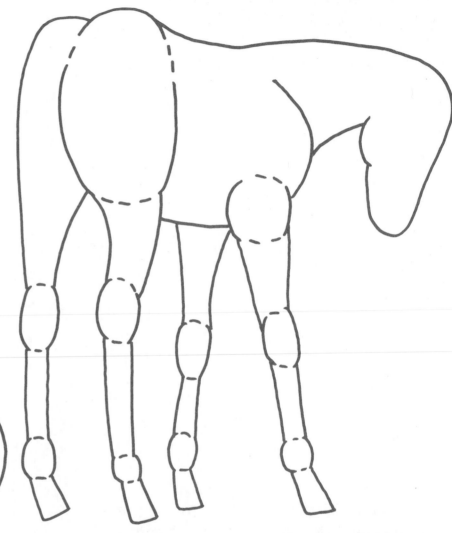

2. Erase unneeded lines in the head and body, then add guideline shapes for the hindquarters and the long, coltish legs. (He will grow into them!)

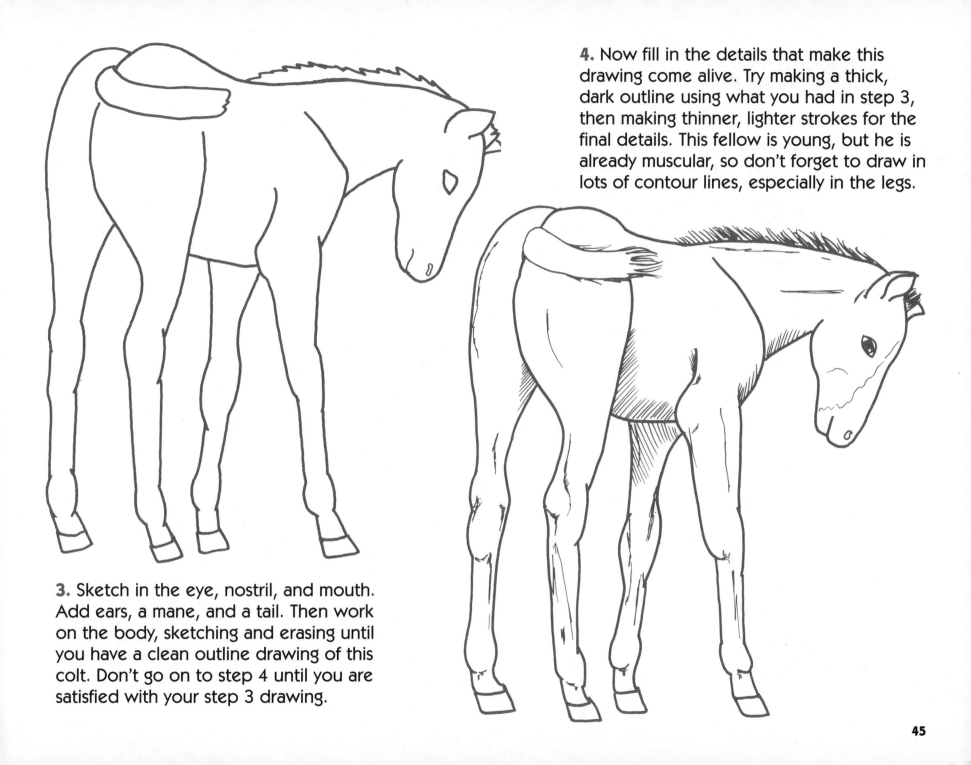

4. Now fill in the details that make this drawing come alive. Try making a thick, dark outline using what you had in step 3, then making thinner, lighter strokes for the final details. This fellow is young, but he is already muscular, so don't forget to draw in lots of contour lines, especially in the legs.

3. Sketch in the eye, nostril, and mouth. Add ears, a mane, and a tail. Then work on the body, sketching and erasing until you have a clean outline drawing of this colt. Don't go on to step 4 until you are satisfied with your step 3 drawing.

Arabian

There is evidence that the Arabian horse existed on the Arabian peninsula as early as 2500 B.C.! Arabians are gentle and affectionate, but known also for their strength and courage. People have used them as warhorses and for long journeys across the desert. The Arabian is often reddish brown with white markings, but it may be a variety of colors, including gray, brown, or black.

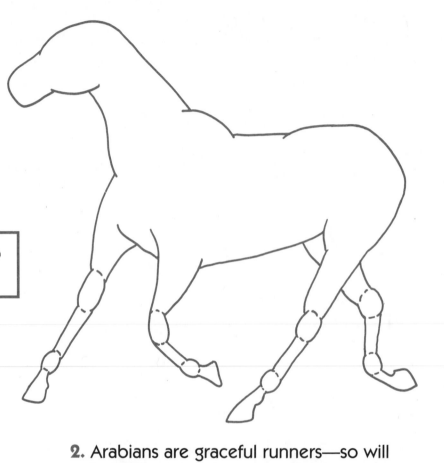

> **Remember**: It usually helps to draw the largest shape first.

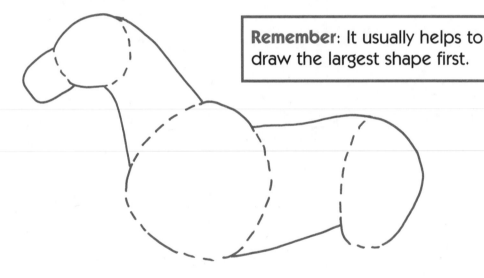

1. Sketch a large, irregular oval for the chest and shoulders. Add narrower, smaller ovals for the head and hindquarters, then connect the ovals and add the muzzle.

2. Arabians are graceful runners—so will yours be, when you are done! Erasing unneeded guidelines, reshape the body and head. Then add the legs. Concentrate on one leg at a time. Then look over your whole drawing. If you are not happy with any part of it, erase that part and try it again. (It is rare to get it right the first time.)

3. Draw in the facial features, ears, windblown mane, and tail. Then go back to work on the legs and body until you have a clean outline drawing you are happy with.

4. Now it is time to add the final details. Think about each one as you add it. Where will you put shading, and why? How about the lines for muscles and skin folds? Can you draw all the mane and tail hairs so they are blowing in the same direction? Paying attention to details will make a good drawing better.

Andalusian

The Andalusian is a breed that originated in Andalusia, a region in southern Spain. Andalusians usually are white or gray, and are known for their ability to learn. During the Middle Ages, this graceful animal was popular with European nobility, and became known as "the royal horse of Europe."

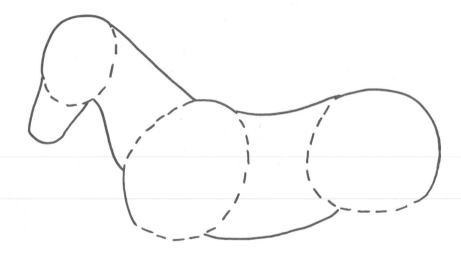

1. For the body, sketch two ovals connected by two curving lines. Draw another oval for the head. Connect the head to the body, then add a guideline shape for the muzzle.

2. Erase the parts of your step 1 ovals that you no longer need, drawing new lines to reshape the body and head. Next, sketch new guideline shapes for the legs and hooves.

Tip: Make sure that you have built a solid foundation in the first two steps before going on to step 3.

3. Work on one area at a time. (Pick the easiest part first.) Add a tail, eyes, nostril, and mouth. Sketch and erase to define the legs and hooves. Then work on refining the head as you add ears and a mane.

4. Now it is time to turn your outline drawing into a realistic-looking Andalusian. Take your time putting in details and finishing touches—contour lines, shading, and color. Use thick lines for what you want to pop out, thin lines for finer details.

Palomino

The golden-coated palomino is found all over the world. It has been popular for centuries—from ancient times, when it was ridden by emperors, kings, and queens, right up to today. The palomino is known for its coloring: a golden or cream-colored coat and a white or pale yellow mane and tail.

Tip: If a drawing seems difficult, don't worry. Be patient. Just take it one step at a time, one area at a time. You *can* do it!

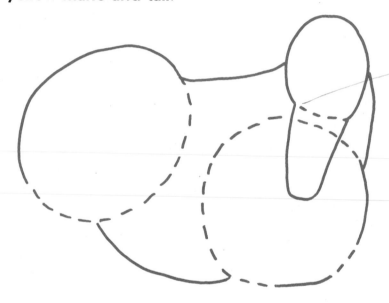

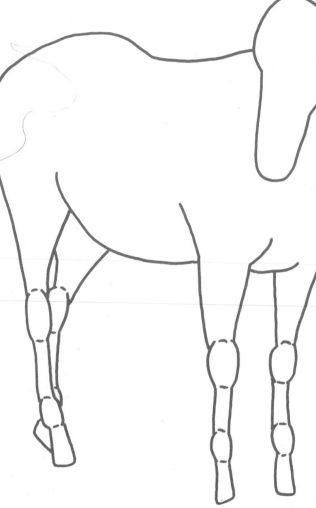

1. Sketching lightly, draw two large ovals for the body, then a smaller one for the head. Connect the ovals as shown. Next, draw a guideline shape for the muzzle. (Note how it overlaps the chest oval.)

2. Erase any unneeded guidelines as you build on the foundation you started in step 1. Reshape the head and body, then create the legs. Take note of which shapes overlap, and why.

3. Add a tail, then work on the legs until you have clean outlines that you are happy with. Then focus on the head, creating ears and a mane, and adding eyes and nostrils.

4. After you add the final details—such as shading and contour lines—polish off your palomino by filling in its trademark colors. (Be sure to leave the face marking white.)

Thoroughbred

The Thoroughbred originated in England in the late 17th or early 18th century. Thoroughbreds are commonly used in organized horse racing, which dates back to 1745 in North America. The Thoroughbred, which often has white markings on the head and legs, is usually reddish brown, gray, or black.

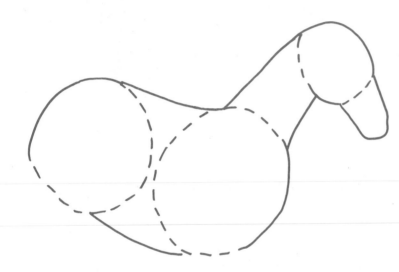

1. Start by drawing guidelines for the body (largest shape first), then do the same for the head. Add a neck and a guideline shape for the muzzle.

Remember: Keep all your lines and shapes lightly drawn until you get to the final stages.

2. Clean up the basic head and body shapes, then start the legs by drawing various-size ovals and connecting lines, as shown.

3. Sketch, erase, and redraw to refine the legs and body, and to start the facial features, ears, mane, and tail. Keep reworking your lines and shapes until you have a clean outline drawing of this horse.

4. Darken the eye, and the flowing mane and tail. Add shading, muscle lines, and other final details. Finish your drawing by coloring in this Thoroughbred—and maybe adding a field or racecourse for it to run on.

Dales Pony

The Dales pony comes from northern England. This strong pony helps farmers and miners carry heavy supplies. It also is used in trotting races, hunting, and the army. The Dales pony is quiet and smart. Its coat is usually black or brown.

1. Sketch guideline shapes for the body and head, then connect them, as shown.

2. Reshape the head and body, erasing unneeded guidelines as you go along. Next, create the legs using basic shapes and simple lines.

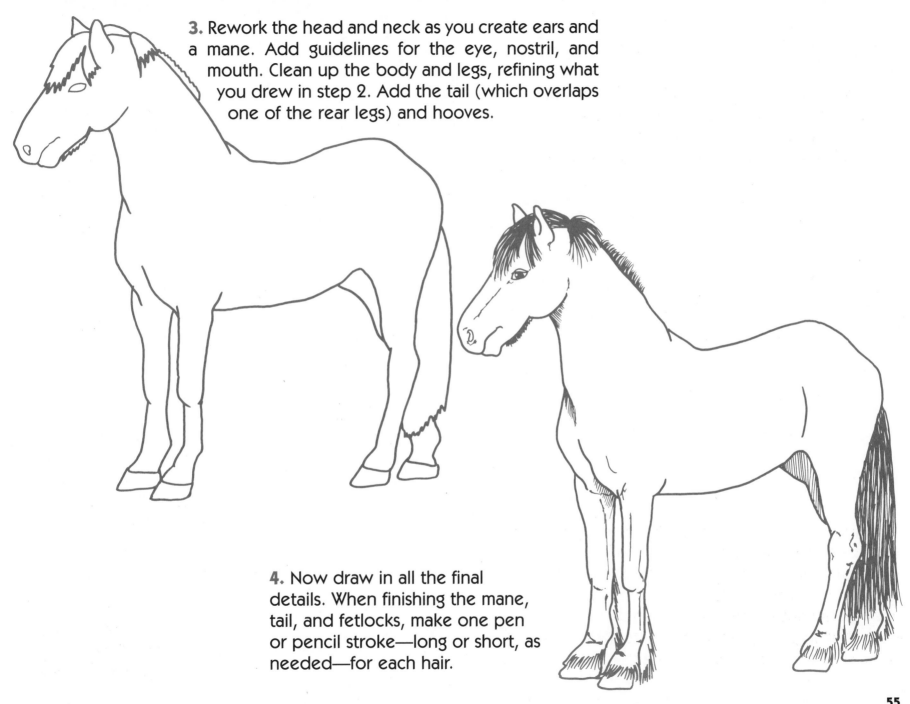

3. Rework the head and neck as you create ears and a mane. Add guidelines for the eye, nostril, and mouth. Clean up the body and legs, refining what you drew in step 2. Add the tail (which overlaps one of the rear legs) and hooves.

4. Now draw in all the final details. When finishing the mane, tail, and fetlocks, make one pen or pencil stroke—long or short, as needed—for each hair.

Barb

The Barb originated in a desert region of North Africa. It is one of the toughest and most enduring horses in the world. Barbs—usually gray in color—can run very fast over short distances.

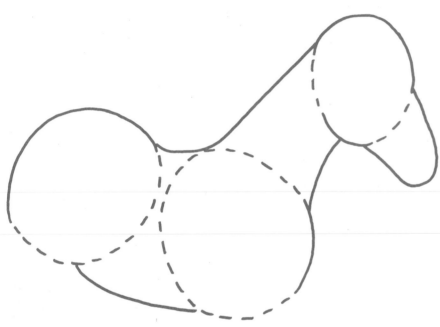

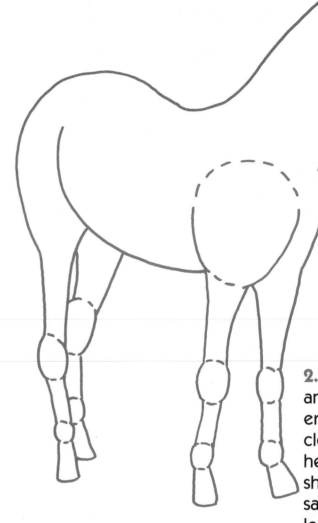

1. Start your drawing with simple guideline shapes—ovals for the chest, hindquarters, and head, plus simple lines for the belly, back, neck, and muzzle. To be sure that your guidelines are where they should be, study the step 4 drawing to see how the basic shapes relate to each other.

2. Draw new lines and shapes and erase old ones to clean up the head-and-body shape. Do the same to create the legs and hooves. Note the new large oval as a guideline for the powerful shoulder.

3. Draw facial features, ears, a mane, and a tail, as shown. Take your time and as you build on your foundation, shaping the legs and body until you have a clean outline drawing of the Barb.

4. Darken the eye, mane, and tail, then add all other finishing touches. Using thick and thin lines, as well as shading and muscle lines, to make your Barb come alive.

Remember: Practice makes perfect. Keep drawing and erasing until you are satisfied with the way your picture looks.

New Forest Pony

This pony is named after a forest in southern England, where the breed originated. Many New Forest ponies still live there, in the wild. Some, however, are being bred and used in competition. The coat is usually a solid color, including brown, reddish brown, and gray. Some have white markings on the head and legs.

Remember: Always use soft, light pencil strokes in a drawing's early stages.

1. Draw a large oval for the chest and shoulder, then a slightly smaller one for the hindquarters. Add curving lines for the back and belly. Then draw a circle for the head, adding lines for the muzzle and neck.

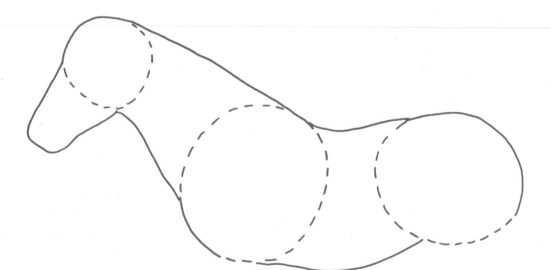

2. Erase unneeded guidelines to clean up the head and body. Start the legs and hooves by drawing ovals of various sizes and connecting them, as shown.

3. Sketch, erase, and redraw lines to create outline shapes for the ears, mane, and facial features. Add the tail. Then work on refining the shape of the legs and hooves, erasing what you don't need as you go along.

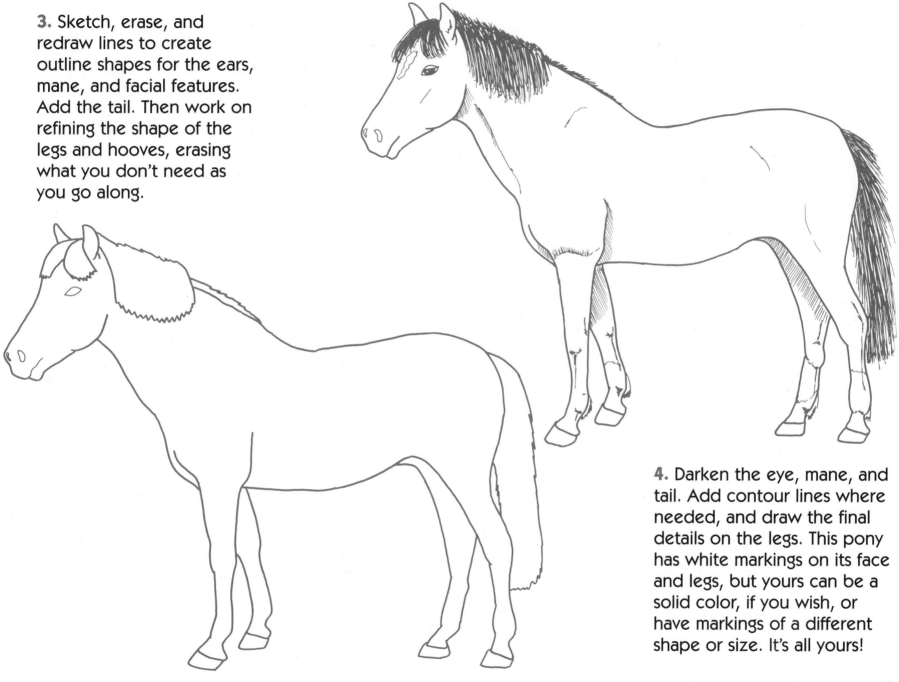

4. Darken the eye, mane, and tail. Add contour lines where needed, and draw the final details on the legs. This pony has white markings on its face and legs, but yours can be a solid color, if you wish, or have markings of a different shape or size. It's all yours!

Lipizzaner

Also called the Lipizzan, this breed came from Lipizza, once a part of the Austro-Hungarian Empire. (Now called Lipica, it is part of Slovenia.) The history of Lipizzaner horses can be traced as far back as the early 1560s. Lipizzaners are born dark brown or black, but turn white or pale gray between the ages of 6 and 10. Most are show horses—the breed is famous for graceful, dancelike performances that include rearing up on its powerful hind legs.

1. Start this horse's head and body by sketching these basic guideline shapes (three ovals) and connecting lines.

2. Now build on what you started. Add ears and legs, erasing unneeded guidelines. Note how lines curve at the jaw, chest, and where the legs join the body.

60

3. Add a mane, tail, facial features, and lines defining the hooves. Keep sketching and erasing until you have a clean outline drawing of the Lipizzaner. Don't go on to step 4 until you are happy with your drawing at this point.

Remember: You can draw almost anything if you first break it down into simple shapes.

4. Add all the final details and finishing touches. Your Lipizzaner will prance right off the page!

Painted Horse

Paint horses, which used to run with buffalo herds and take part in cattle drives in the Old West, were popular with Native Americans and cowboys alike. The paint horse is very similar to the pinto—both have the *overo* or the *tobiano* coloring *(see page 20)*. However, a paint is bred from paint horses, quarter horses, and Thoroughbreds only. A pinto can come from crossing a number of various breeds.

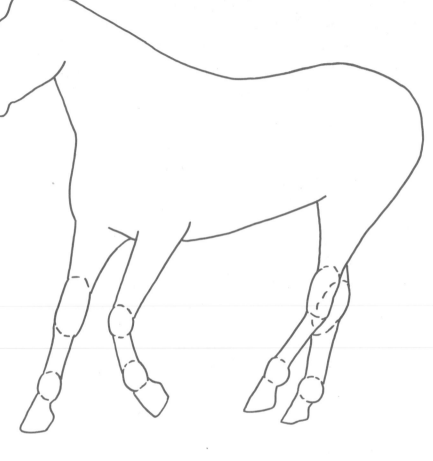

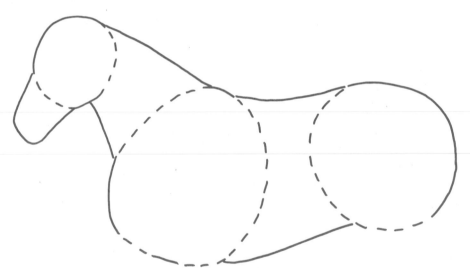

1. Sketch a big oval for this horse's powerful chest and shoulders. Adding a smaller oval and connecting the two shapes form the body. A smaller oval and some simple lines start the horse's head and neck.

2. Clean up the head and body shapes, erasing guidelines you don't need. Add the legs, sketching and erasing to get each leg in the position shown.

3. Create ears, a mane, facial features, a tail, and hooves. Then clean up your drawing. Darken all the lines you want to keep, and erase the rest.

4. Add the final details. Have fun making the brushy mane! Don't forget shading and muscle lines. When you are ready to color the coat, you can use our markings or design your own. Will your painted horse be an *overo* or a *tobiano*?

Percheron

The Percheron originated in the Perche region of France. It has served as a warhorse, coach horse, farm horse, and riding horse. Today, Percherons are used for recreation—hayrides, sleighrides, and parades. Most Percherons are black or gray.

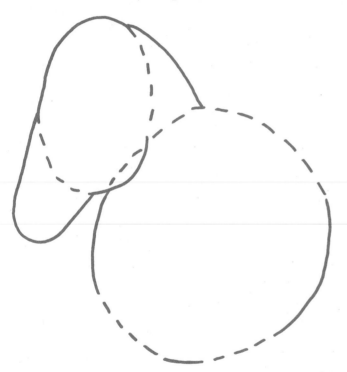

1. Make a large oval for this horse's body. For the head, add a smaller oval overlapping the body shape, then draw guidelines for the muzzle and neck.

2. Erase the lines that are dotted in step 1. Then add two ovals that overlap the body shape, as shown. Then add simple shapes for the legs and hooves.

Remember: Don't be afraid to erase. Revising is an important part of the process. Make the job easier by keeping your pencil lines light and softly drawn.

3. Create a mane and ears as you refine the shape of this horse's body. Then add facial features, legs, and hooves. This horse is facing you, so use fore-shortening to make it look more realistic. Foreshortening is when you make what is closer to you larger than what is farther away. Though all four legs are the same size, draw the rear legs shorter so they will look farther away.

4. Complete the mane, ears, and facial features. Add a fringe of hair above each hoof. Draw all the small lines that show how muscular this horse's legs and body are. Add shading to give your picture depth. Last but not least, color your Percheron. This one has spots, but yours can be a solid color, with or with-out a mark on its head.

Clydesdale

This horse gets its name from Scotland's Clyde River Valley, where it originated. It is now found throughout Scotland and northern England, and there are some in North America. The Clydesdale is usually reddish brown, dark brown, or black, with white markings on its head and white "stockings" on its legs. It is about 66 inches tall and can weigh up to a ton!

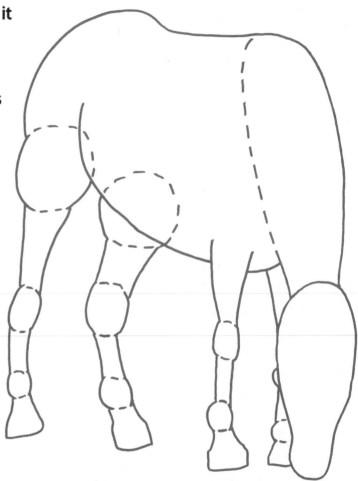

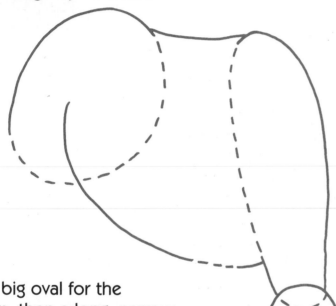

1. Sketch a big oval for the hindquarters, then a long, narrow one for the neck. (This horse has its head down.) Connect the two ovals with curving lines for the back and belly. (The belly line overlaps the rear oval.) Add guideline shapes for the head and muzzle.

2. Erase guidelines for the head and hindquarters. Next, using soft, light pencil strokes, draw guideline shapes for the legs and hooves. Get everything here the way you want it before moving to the next step.

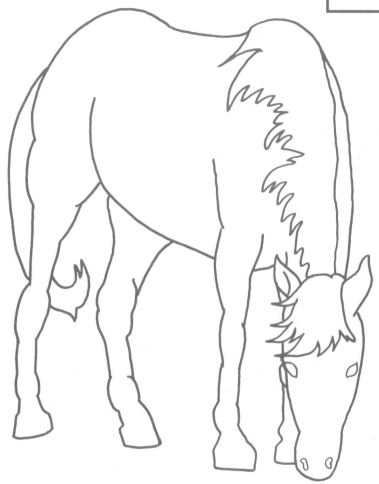

3. Create a tail, mane, ears, eyes, and nostrils. Keep erasing old lines and sketching new ones as you rework the leg and body shapes into a smooth outline.

4. Have some fun adding all the final details, such as the long, thick hair on the lower legs—a Clydesdale trademark.

Welsh Cob

In the 1400s, British knights rode Welsh cob ponies into battle. Later, farmers used them as work animals. Today, these beautiful animals are often seen at jumping competitions. Welsh cob ponies can be a number of colors, including black, brown, dun (a grayish yellow), and white.

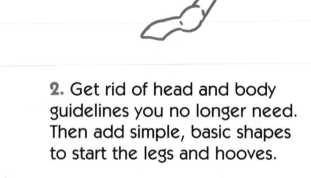

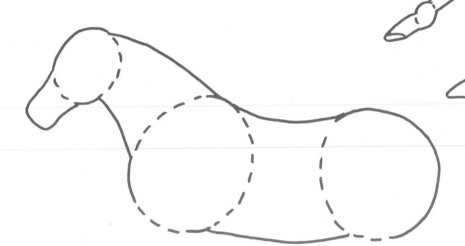

1. Start this pony with the basic head and body shapes: ovals connected by curving lines.

2. Get rid of head and body guidelines you no longer need. Then add simple, basic shapes to start the legs and hooves.

Remember: Take your time with steps 1 and 2. If you get the foundation right, the rest will be easy to do.

3. Refine all the parts of your drawing (one area at a time!) to make a clean outline drawing of this Welsh cob. This pony is running, so make its mane and tail look windblown.

4. Darken the eye, mane, and tail. Then add shading, contour lines, and other finishing touches. Once you are done, your pony can run free!

Connemara

The Connemara is a gentle, friendly pony named after the area in western Ireland from which it comes. The Connemara can be almost any color, but usually is gray, black, or brown. This pony is an excellent jumper and hunter.

Remember: It takes patience, practice, and a lot of erasing and sketching to get a drawing just right.

2. Erase old guidelines to clean up the head and body. Then draw new guidelines to add legs and hooves.

1. Lightly draw your first guideline shapes—two large ovals for the body, and a smaller one for the head. Connecting the ovals with simple lines, as shown, gives this pony a muzzle, neck, back, and belly.

70

3. Again, erase old guidelines as you add new parts. This time, it is ears, a mane, facial features, hooves, and a tail. Erase and redraw as much as you need to, until you have a clean outline drawing that you are happy with.

4. Refine the ears and facial features, then add details that will make the mane, tail, body, and legs look more realistic. For finishing touches, you may want to color your pony, or add a background scene.

Mustang

The mustang comes from Spain and was brought to the Americas by the Spanish. Today, these horses still run wild in parts of the western United States. Mustangs can be found in almost every horse color, solid or pattern.

1. Because of the angle we are viewing this horse from, the oval for the chest and shoulder is much bigger than the one for the hindquarters. Connect those two shapes, then draw a circle for the head, adding shapes for the muzzle and neck.

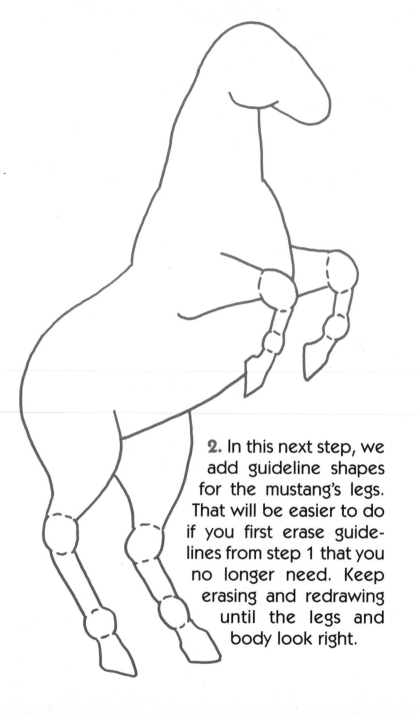

2. In this next step, we add guideline shapes for the mustang's legs. That will be easier to do if you first erase guidelines from step 1 that you no longer need. Keep erasing and redrawing until the legs and body look right.

3. Give your mustang a mane and ears. Add eyes, a nostril, mouth, and tail. Then spend some time reworking every part of the horse, one area at a time, until you have a clean, clear outline drawing that you are happy with.

Remember: Do not start adding fine details until your step 3 drawing is complete and satisfactory.

4. Once you have the basic size and shape right, adding little details can make your drawing really work. By adjusting an angle, rounding out a curve, or adding some shading, you can make a good drawing better.

Norwegian Fjord

The Norwegian Fjord *(fee-ORD)* is one of the world's oldest horse breeds. It almost always is cream-colored and has a dark stripe, called an eel stripe, down its back. The Vikings used this strong pony when they went to war, and European farmers used it as a work animal. Today, it is used for pleasure riding as well as work.

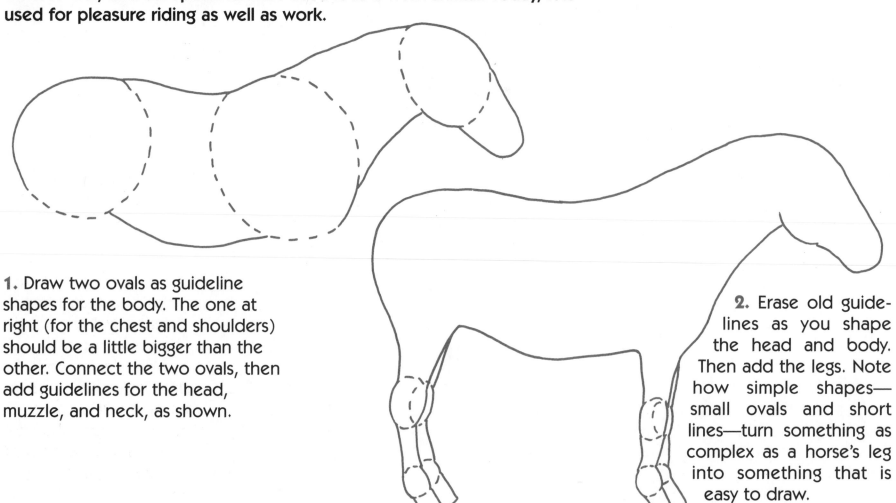

1. Draw two ovals as guideline shapes for the body. The one at right (for the chest and shoulders) should be a little bigger than the other. Connect the two ovals, then add guidelines for the head, muzzle, and neck, as shown.

2. Erase old guidelines as you shape the head and body. Then add the legs. Note how simple shapes—small ovals and short lines—turn something as complex as a horse's leg into something that is easy to draw.

3. Reshape the head slightly to make room for ears and a mane. Add facial features, hooves, and a tail. Erase old guidelines, and keep revising until you have made a clean, smooth outline drawing of this pony.

Remember: Once you are satisfied with your step 3 drawing, use a fine-point pen or marker over lines you want to keep. This will make it easier to erase any old guidelines that remain.

4. Now that your outline is ready, start filling it in. Final details include darkening the eye, mane, and tail. Small lines for muscles or skin folds will give the drawing depth. Put in a little shading, and you are done!

American Standardbred

The American Standardbred is the fastest harness racehorse in the world! Its ancestor is the Thoroughbred. The Standardbred is a little shorter than the Thoroughbred, with a longer body. Most Standardbreds are bay (reddish brown, with a black mane and tail), black, or brown, but some have other horse colorings.

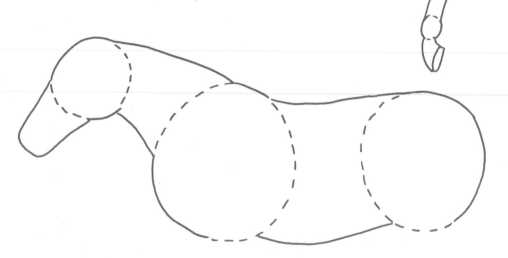

1. Use soft, light pencil strokes to draw guideline ovals for the body and head. Do the same when adding guidelines for the muzzle, neck, back, and belly.

2. Clean up the head and body shapes, then draw guidelines for the legs and hooves. Work on one leg at a time. When all four are done, look at the overall drawing. Erase and redraw anything that doesn't fit. There is no need to rush—this isn't a race!

3. Add ears, mane, facial features, and tail. Clean and refine the shape of each leg. Go over each part of your drawing, one area at a time, until you have a clean outline drawing that works.

Remember: You can draw almost anything if you break it down into simple steps.

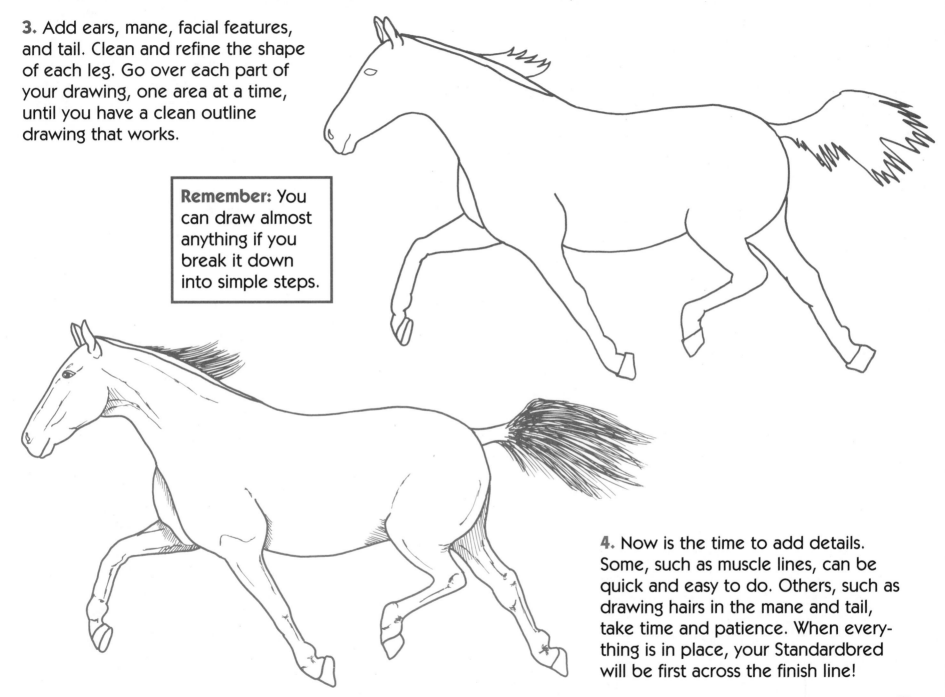

4. Now is the time to add details. Some, such as muscle lines, can be quick and easy to do. Others, such as drawing hairs in the mane and tail, take time and patience. When everything is in place, your Standardbred will be first across the finish line!

Russian Trotter

As you might guess from its name, this breed originated in Russia. A sport horse, its specialty is harness racing—it can run the 1,600-meter course (a little less than a mile) in under two minutes! The colors most common to this breed are chestnut, bay, and black. Some are gray.

Remember: Dotted lines represent guidelines that you will erase later, when you no longer need them.

1. Draw a large oval, then a slightly smaller one next to it. Connect them to start the body. Next, draw a circle for the head. Add simple lines for the muzzle and neck.

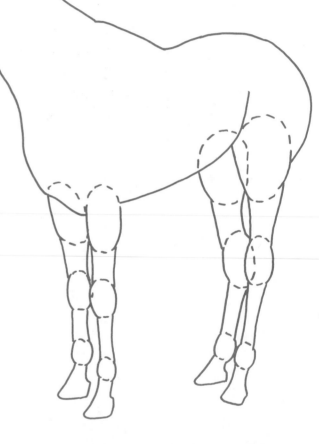

2. Clean up the head and body shapes, then add guidelines for the legs and hooves, as shown.

3. Work on creating a clean, smooth outline drawing of this horse. As you erase old guide-lines and fine-tune the shape of others, add ears, a mane and tail, facial features, and hooves. Note where lines curve or straighten, and how shapes and sizes relate to each other.

4. Have fun adding the finishing touches, but take care with them. Contour lines, shading, color, and other details all contribute to a successful drawing!

Mule

A mule is half horse, half donkey. (Sometimes, the word *mule* is used for the offspring of a male horse and a female donkey, and *hinny* for the offspring of a female horse and a male donkey.) The mule is one of the best work animals. It is strong and brave, yet calm, and can work longer than horses. Mules can be any of the same colors and markings as horses, except paint.

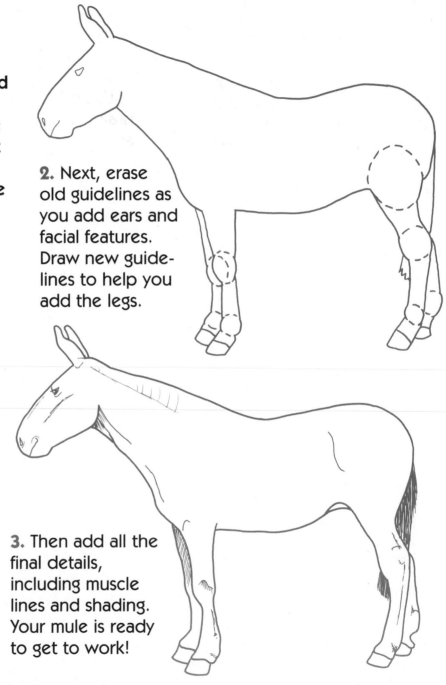

2. Next, erase old guidelines as you add ears and facial features. Draw new guidelines to help you add the legs.

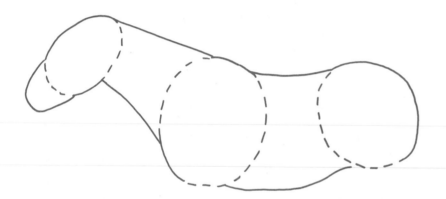

1. Try drawing this animal in three steps instead of four. First, sketch guideline shapes for the head and body, then connect them, as shown.

3. Then add all the final details, including muscle lines and shading. Your mule is ready to get to work!

Remember: Keep all lines lightly drawn, so they will be easy to erase.

Padang

The Padang is a breed of pony originating in Sumatra, Indonesia. (*Padang* is the name of a river and a city, as well as a pony.) This calm, easygoing animal is brown or bay.

1. Use light strokes to draw three ovals to serve as guideline shapes for the body and head. Connect them as shown.

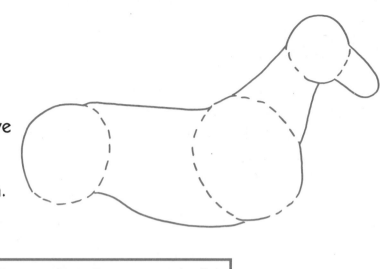

Remember: Be sure to build a good foundation before refining your drawing.

2. Erase and redraw as needed to add ears, mane, facial features, and tail. Then start the legs.

3. Erase all leftover guidelines. Once you have a clean outline, fill in all the details.

Zebra

Zebras are not horses, but they are closely related and look very much alike—except for the zebra's famous black and white stripes. The zebra once lived throughout Africa, Asia, Europe, and North America. Today, it is found mostly in southern Africa.

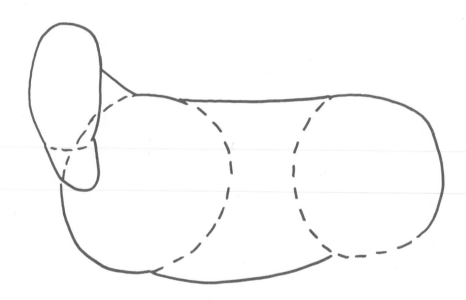

1. Draw two large ovals, making the one at left a little larger than the other. Connect them to form the zebra's body. Then draw a narrow oval for the head and add a U for the muzzle. This zebra is looking sideways, so the head and muzzle shapes overlap the chest oval. Add a line for the neck.

2. Erase lines you don't need to get a clearer picture of the head and body. Add legs. You will see that each leg is made of two or three ovals, which get smaller as you go down. (Looking over at the step 4 drawing will help you understand where each shape goes, and why.)

3. Add ears, a mane, facial features, and a tail. Reshape the head and body until they look right to you. Do the same for each leg, adding a line for the hoof.

4. Ready to go wild? A zebra needs its stripes, but tackle them last. First, take care of all the other details: ears, face, mane, and tail, plus shading and muscle lines. When you have them the way you want them, add those stripes!

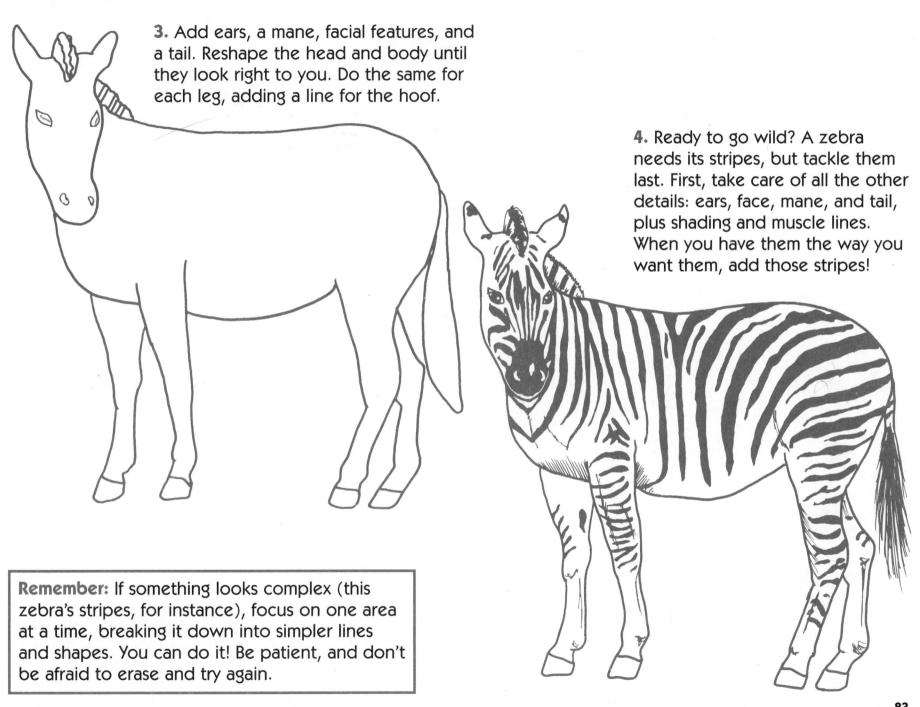

Remember: If something looks complex (this zebra's stripes, for instance), focus on one area at a time, breaking it down into simpler lines and shapes. You can do it! Be patient, and don't be afraid to erase and try again.

Belgian Heavy Draft

Also known as the Brabant, this horse is used mostly for farming or pulling wagons. Its stocky body and muscular legs give it the power to haul heavy weights. (*Draft* means "used for pulling loads.") It may be one of several horse colors, but usually is roan *(see page 40)* or reddish brown, with a white or yellow mane and tail.

(see page 40)

Remember: Keep all lines light and softly drawn until the final stages.

1. Start by drawing a large oval for this horse's powerful chest and shoulder. Draw a slightly smaller one for its hindquarters, then connect the two ovals. Draw another oval for the head, then add simple lines to start the muzzle and neck.

2. Erase unneeded lines from the head and body shapes, making one clean outline. Then sketch guideline shapes for the legs and hooves.

3. Erase and redraw the head and neck lines to create a mouth, ears, and a mane. Add an eye and nostril. Clean and reshape the legs. You should have a clean outline drawing of this horse before going to the last step.

4. Now add the details that make this horse ready for action. Note the muscle lines in its shoulder and legs. Don't forget the tufts of hair on the lower legs!

Camargue

In the wild, the Camargue *(kah-MARG)* lives in the marshes of southern France. (The horse and its home area are now protected by the government.) The Camargue is born black or brown, usually with a white forehead mark. As an adult, it is pale gray.

1. Start the body by drawing two ovals and connecting them, as shown. Add two narrower ovals to start the head and muzzle, then draw neck lines.

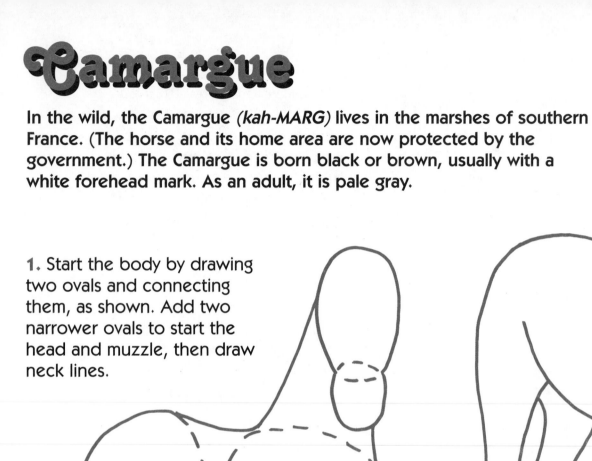

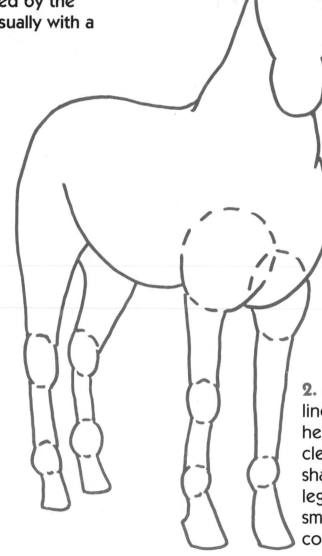

2. Erase old guidelines to make the head and body a clean outline shape. Start the legs by drawing small ovals and connecting them.

3. Reshape the head to define the muzzle and add eyes, ears, and the mane. Put in the nostrils. Then reshape the body and legs, adding hooves and a tail. Erase all unneeded guidelines to form a clean outline drawing.

4. This step will keep your pencil busy for a while. You have a lot of details to add here: lines to highlight the muscles and other body curves, shading to add depth, and the long, silky hairs in the mane and tail. Before you know it, a Camargue will be gazing back at you!

Remember: Focus on one part of the body at a time. Keep drawing and erasing until you are satisfied before moving on to the next part.

Marwari

This brave and loyal horse, which comes from the Marwar region of India, was ridden into battle in medieval times. It can walk in sand and go long periods on little water, making it a good ride for desert dwellers. The Marwari has unusual ears—they curl inward, sometimes even touching each other! Most Marwaris are brown, reddish brown, or cream-colored, with large blotches of white.

Remember: Practice makes perfect! Don't be discouraged if you don't get the hang of it right away. Just keep drawing and erasing until you do.

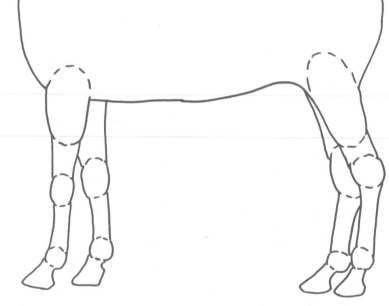

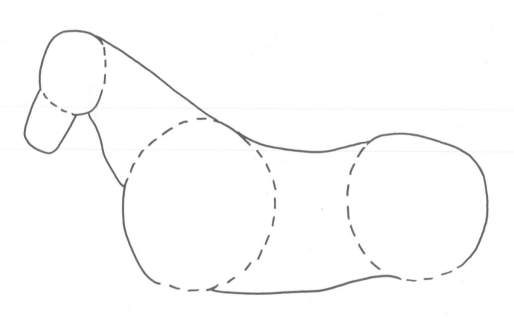

1. Using light pencil strokes, draw two big ovals (one a little smaller than the other). Connect them to form the basic body shape. Add an oval and other guidelines for the head, neck, and muzzle.

2. Building on what you drew in step 1, reshape the head and body, erasing old guidelines as you work. Then draw ovals connected by lines to start the legs and hooves.

3. Draw curving triangles for the distinctive Marwari ears. Add guidelines for the mane and facial features. Put in hooves and the tail. Then erase and redraw lines until the shapes of the head, body, and legs are just the way you want them.

4. Now add all the finishing touches, including muscle lines, mane and tail, and shading. Then outline the body markings and color them in. (Your Marwari's markings can be different from ours.) When you are done, step back and admire your work!

Scenery

Want to give your horses and ponies a setting where they would feel at home? Use this one, or create your own.